Contents

Christmas

Ho, ho, ho!

Christmas is a Christian festival that celebrates the birth of Jesus about 2,000 years ago. Christians believe that Jesus was the Son of God. The story of the birth of Jesus is called the **Nativity**. Christmas Day is celebrated on 25 December. The four-week period before Christmas is called **Advent**. This is when people prepare to celebrate the birth of Jesus. They sing special songs, called **carols**, and decorate their homes. After Christmas Day, Christians in some countries celebrate the 12 Days of Christmas, ending on 6 January.

At Christmas people use brightly coloured decorations, such as baubles and stars, to hang on Christmas trees, and to decorate their homes and workplaces.

ORIGAMI
FESTIVALS

Robyn Hardyman

W
FRANKLIN WATTS
LONDON • SYDNEY

Franklin Watts
First published in Great Britain in 2016 by The Watts Publishing Group

Credits
Series Editors: Sarah Eason and Jennifer Sanderson
Series Designer: Jessica Moon
All origami photography by Jessica Moon

Picture credits: Cover: Shutterstock: Alice Daniel, Fotohunter, Mara008, USBFCO. Inside: Shutterstock: Africa Studio 4–5, Marilyn Barbone 19, Beata Becla 18–19, Alice Daniel throughout, Christopher Elwell 12–13, Fotohunter throughout, Nicole Gordine 25, Graphic-line 6–7, Mara008 throughout, Vladimir Melnikov 24–25, Rena Schild 13, Small1 7, USBFCO throughout, Xenia_ok throughout.

HB ISBN: 978 1 4451 5063 5
PB ISBN: 978 1 4451 5064 2

Printed in China

Franklin Watts
An imprint of
Hachette Children's Group
Part of The Watts Publishing Group
Carmelite House
50 Victoria Embankment
London EC4Y 0DZ

An Hachette UK Company
www.hachette.co.uk

www.franklinwatts.co.uk

Folds, Bases and Paper

These instructions explain the main folds and bases you will use. The activities are rated from 1 to 5 to show level of difficulty.

Valley fold: To make a valley fold, fold the paper towards you.

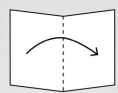

- - - - - - - - - - - - - - -

Mountain fold: To make a mountain fold, fold the paper away from you.

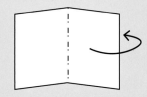

- · - · - · - · - · - · - · -

 Turn the model over   Rotate the model

 Cut with scissors   Push or pull in this direction

Square Base

  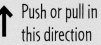

Blintz Base

Inside/Outside Reverse Folds

 Inside    Outside

---

Celebrating Christmas

Today, Christians all around the world celebrate Christmas. They remember the Nativity story, they go to church and they give cards and gifts to their families and friends. Many people who are not Christians also celebrate with their families and friends at Christmas time. It is a holiday from work and a time to enjoy the company of loved ones. People join together to eat special meals and to exchange gifts. Cities, towns and villages have their streets decorated with colourful decorations and lights.

In this book you will find out how to make some wonderful origami pieces that will make Christmas even more fun and festive!

Waterbomb Base

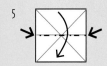

Squash Fold

Paper: You can use almost any kind of paper, but you can also buy origami paper from craft shops.

The Christmas Story

About 2,000 years ago, in a place called Judea (part of Israel), God sent an **angel** called Gabriel to tell a young woman, Mary, that she would have a special baby, a boy called Jesus. Jesus would be the Son of God.

Mary married a **carpenter** called Joseph, and together, they travelled to the town of Bethlehem. When they arrived it was crowded and there was nowhere for them to stay. An innkeeper gave them a place in his stable. This is where the baby Jesus was born. Mary laid the baby in a **manger**, or trough, full of hay.

Follow the Star

Nearby, some shepherds out on the hills with their sheep suddenly saw a bright star in the night sky. An angel sent by God told them to follow the star to Bethlehem, to find Jesus. They did this, and found the baby in the stable. Far away to the east, three wise men, or kings, also saw a new star in the sky. They also followed the star, and after 12 days they came to Bethlehem, where they found Jesus, Mary and Joseph in the stable.

The wise men were called Gaspar, Melchior and Balthazar.

The Nativity Star

Stars are often used as decorations at Christmas time. The Nativity star reminds us of the star of Bethlehem that the shepherds and wise men saw.

Christmas Crown

This Christmas crown will remind you of the three wise men who travelled to see Jesus in Bethlehem.

1 Place a large piece of paper coloured side down. Valley fold in half from the top to the bottom and then unfold.

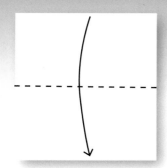

2 Valley fold your paper in half from the left to the right, and then unfold.

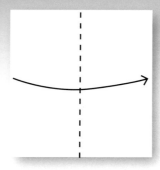

3 Valley fold all four corners into the centre of your model.

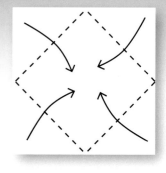

4 Your model should now look like this. Turn over your model and rotate it by 45 degrees.

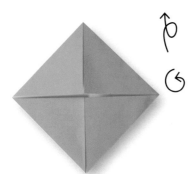

5 Your model should now look like this. Valley fold your model in half from the top to the bottom, and then unfold.

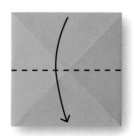

6 Valley fold the top and bottom of your model into the centre.

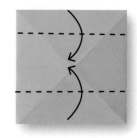

7 Your model should now look like this. Valley fold the top triangle down to the bottom.

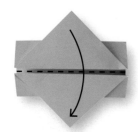

8 Valley fold the top left and top right corners into the centre.

9 Fold both triangle layers to the top.

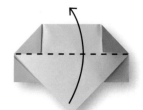

8

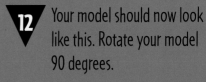

10 Valley fold the left and right corners into the middle.

11 Now fold the upper triangle layer back down.

12 Your model should now look like this. Rotate your model 90 degrees.

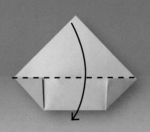

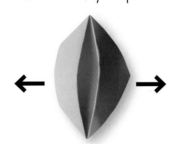

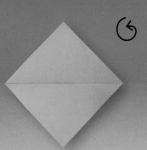

13 Gently open up your model.

14 Your model should now look like this. Keep opening up your model, smoothing out the inside as you open it.

15 Shape the four corners of the crown using your fingers. Your crown is now ready to wear.

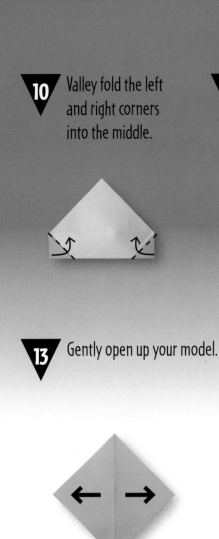

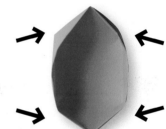

To make a larger crown, use a bigger piece of paper.

Shining Star

Make lots of these origami Christmas stars to decorate a room or tree. You could also use them as gift tags.

LEVEL OF DIFFICULTY 3

1 Start with the coloured side of your paper facing down. Valley fold your paper in half, from the top to the bottom.

2 Valley fold the left and right points down to the bottom, and then unfold.

3 Valley fold the right side over to the left.

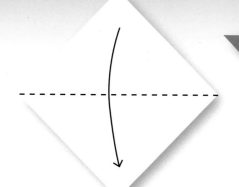

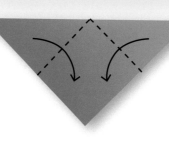

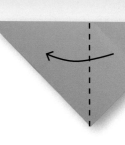

4 Valley fold the upper layer back over to the right.

5 Your model should now look like this. Turn over your model.

6 Now valley fold the right side over to the left.

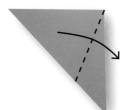

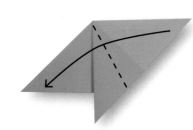

7 Pull the right inner layer out to the right.

8 Valley fold the upper left side over to the right.

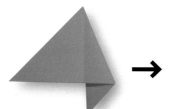

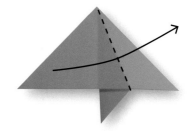

10

9 Valley fold down the top right point.

10 Valley fold the upper layer of the bottom points.

11 Your model should now look like this. Turn over your model.

12 Your model should now look like this. Valley fold the right side over to the left.

13 Valley fold the lower left point over to the right.

14 Your star is now complete. Rotate slightly so the upper point is at the top.

Make a hole at the top of your star and thread some ribbon through it. Hang the star on your Christmas tree.

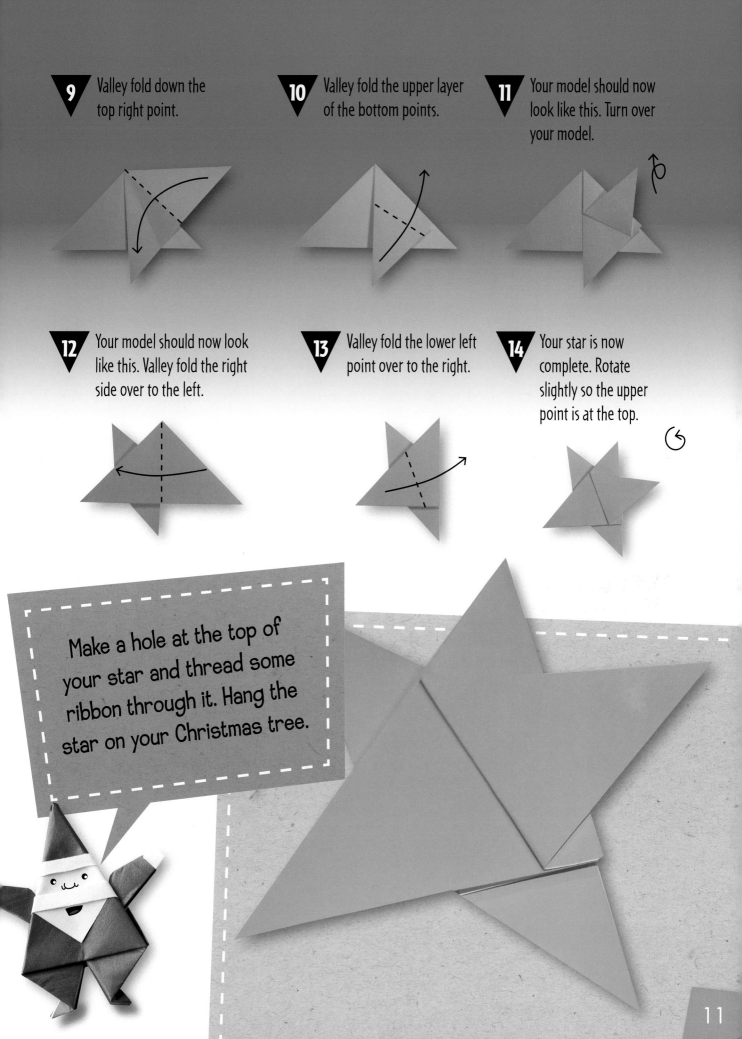

Festive Trees

At Christmas, people put a fir tree, pine tree or artificial tree indoors and decorate it with shiny decorations and lights. At the top, they place either a star or an angel. This **tradition** comes from long ago, before Christian times, when people used branches from **evergreen** trees to decorate their homes in mid-winter. It made them think of the spring.

Decorating the tree is a great way to get into a festive mood at Christmas time.

You can hang just about anything you like on your Christmas tree to make it really sparkle and shine.

Modern Trees

In the sixteenth century, people in Germany began the **custom** of decorating a fir tree indoors at Christmas. Trees were decorated with foods, such as fruits and nuts, and with many small candles. In the 1800s, the custom spread to the United Kingdom and the United States. Having candles on trees was dangerous because the trees can catch fire. In 1895, the first electric Christmas lights were invented, and today people love to string coloured or white lights on their tree to make it pretty.

Ho, ho, ho!

National Christmas Trees

This tree near the White House in Washington, DC, is decorated each year at Christmas time. This is a custom that has taken place since 1923. In December each year, the President of the United States turns on the Christmas tree lights, marking the beginning of the festive season.

Candy Canes

Tinsel and candy canes are both often hung on Christmas trees. This tradition comes from Germany. The story is that candy canes were invented to keep children happy during long Christmas services in church. In 1957, a machine that curled candy canes automatically, instead of by hand, was invented. It was called the Keller machine.

Christmas Tree

This Christmas tree is so easy to make you could make a whole forest of them! You could use them as Christmas cards for your friends and family.

LEVEL OF DIFFICULTY
5

1 Start with a square base, open points at the bottom.

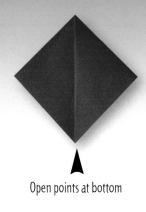

Open points at bottom

2 Fold the upper left layer to the centre, and then unfold.

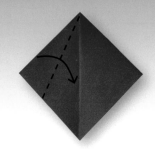

3 Now lift the upper left layer to the centre and open slightly.

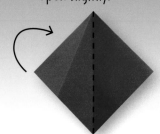

4 Press down to flatten the flap. This is called a squash fold.

5 Fold the rear left layer to the centre and then open slightly.

6 Perform another squash fold to flatten the flap.

7 Your model should now look like this. Turn over your model.

8 Your model should now look like this. Repeat steps 2 to 6 on this side of your model.

9 Your model should look like this. Fold the upper left layer over to the right.

14

10 Your model should now look like this. Turn over the model.

 11 Fold the upper left layer over to the right.

 12 Your model should now look like this on both sides. Valley fold the entire bottom section up, and then unfold.

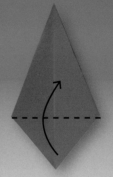

 13 Carefully tuck the upper layer of the bottom section up and under the top triangle section. Repeat on the remaining triangle flaps.

14 Your model should now look like this. Carefully open the model to create the Christmas tree shape.

15 Repeat steps 1 to 14 on two smaller pieces of paper, staggered in size. Place the largest tree at the bottom, then stagger them until the smallest is placed at the top.

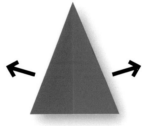

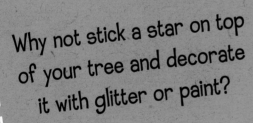

Why not stick a star on top of your tree and decorate it with glitter or paint?

15

Candy Cane

This paper candy cane will look amazing on your tree, but it will not taste as good as the real thing!

LEVEL OF DIFFICULTY 2

1 Start with your paper coloured side down. Valley fold the bottom point up towards the top, but not quite reaching the top.

2 Your model should now look like this. Turn over your model.

3 Valley fold the bottom up the same distance that you left from the top point in step 1.

4 Again, valley fold the bottom up the same distance as in step 1.

5 Continue to fold until you have reached the top of your paper. This will probably take about three or four folds.

6 Your model should now look like this. Rotate your model 90 degrees.

7 Valley fold in the ends of your model to remove the points.

8 Valley fold the model to the right, just above halfway.

9 Valley fold the model down to create the hook of the candy cane.

10 Your candy cane is now complete.

Make a few candy canes to decorate your Christmas tree or display them in a jar on a table.

Giving Gifts

In the Christmas story, the three wise men brought gifts to the baby Jesus. At Christmas, people give gifts to their loved ones to remember the gifts of the wise men, and the gift that God gave of his son, Jesus. Different countries have different traditions for gift-giving. In the United States and the United Kingdom, children leave out stockings on Christmas Eve. On Christmas morning these are full of presents to open. In many European countries, the presents are left in shoes or boots. Adults often leave each other gifts under the Christmas tree.

Choose brightly coloured gift wrap and boxes to make your parcels look beautiful when placed under the tree.

The Gifts of the Wise Men

The wise men brought gold (middle), frankincense (bottom) and myrrh (top) for Jesus. Gold is a precious metal that was given to kings. Frankincense is a kind of perfume. It was used in Jewish worship, so it showed the holiness of Jesus. Myrrh is another perfume, and was used to make dead bodies smell pleasant. It showed that Jesus would suffer when he grew up to be a man.

Secret Santa

A popular way to give gifts to people in a group such as a school class is to have a 'Secret Santa'. People write their names on a piece of paper, and these are put in a container. Each person draws out one name and must buy a present for that person. The gifts are given anonymously. This means no-one knows who has given which gift – it is a secret!

Don't tell!

Gift Box

This box is perfect for giving a small gift or some sweets. Make the bottom from a slightly smaller piece of paper than the top, so the top will fit over the bottom.

LEVEL OF DIFFICULTY
4

1 To make the top, start with a blintz base and the paper colour side down. Unfold your base so that your paper lies flat again.

2 Valley fold the four corners of your paper into the first fold lines created by your blintz base.

3 Valley fold the corners in again along the folds created by the base.

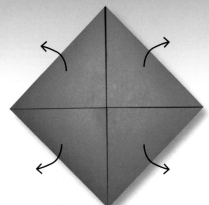

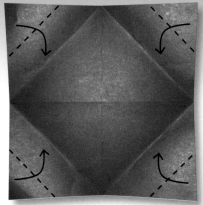

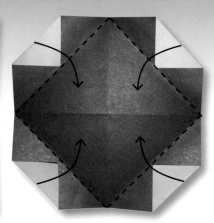

4 Your model should now look like this. Turn over your model and rotate it by 45 degrees.

5 Valley fold the left and right sides into the centre.

6 Fold the upper left layer of paper over to the right.

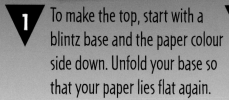

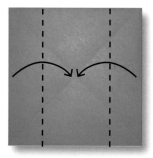

7 Valley fold the top and bottom left corners into the centre.

8 Fold the upper right layer of paper back to the left side.

Do the same to the other side by valley folding the upper right layer of paper over to the left.

Valley fold the top and bottom right corners into the centre.

Fold the upper left layer of paper back to the right side.

12 Gently open your box by pulling the top layers up and out.

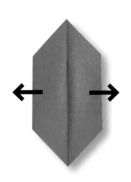

13 Once open, shape the corners to create the four sides of your square box.

14 The top of your box is now complete. To create the bottom of your box, repeat steps 1 to 13 using a slightly smaller piece of paper.

Why not try using different coloured or patterned paper for the top and bottom?

Happy Christmas! x x x

Gift Bow

Decorate a gift with this lovely bow and impress your friends and family. You can use gift wrap to make it extra Christmassy!

1 To make your gift bow, start with a blintz base. Valley fold all four corners into the centre.

2 Your model should now look like this. Turn over your model.

3 Valley fold all four corners into the centre.

4 Valley fold each triangle section outwards, so the tips of the triangles overlap the edges of the square.

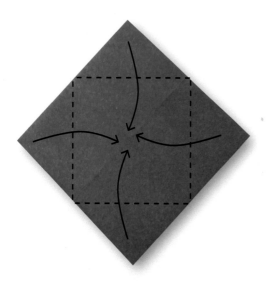

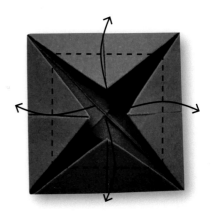

5 Your model should now look like this. Turn over your model.

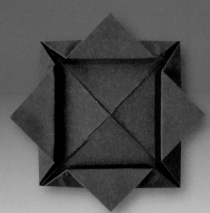

6 Valley fold the upper layer of the triangles outwards. Crease along the fold but do not press the triangles flat. Allow them to stick up.

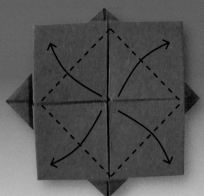

7 Valley fold the next layer of triangles outwards. Crease the paper along the fold but do not press the triangles flat. Allow them to stick up.

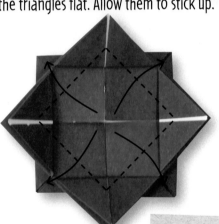

8 Your finished bow should look like this.

Use a bigger piece of paper to make a larger bow and write a special message in the middle.

Happy Christmas! xxx

Santa Claus

At Christmas, a special gift-giver visits each home and brings gifts to children. In many countries, the best-known gift-bringer is **Santa Claus**, or **Father Christmas**. Some countries have different traditions. In many Spanish-speaking countries, for example, the gift-bearer is the baby Jesus himself.

Santa's sleigh is pulled by nine reindeer: Dasher, Dancer, Prancer, Vixen, Comet, Cupid, Donner, Blitzen and Rudolf.

Saint Nicholas

The man behind the story of Santa Claus is **Saint Nicholas**. He was a rich and generous **bishop**. The story tells of a poor man who did not have enough money to have his three daughters married. Nicholas secretly dropped a bag of gold down his chimney. The man saw it fall into a stocking that had been hung up to dry. When this happened a second time, the man hid to see who was dropping the gold. He caught Nicholas on the third time, then told his friends the story. Then, when anyone received a secret gift, they said it was from Nicholas!

Saint Nicholas' Day

In the Netherlands, Saint Nicholas is known as **Sinterklaas**. He brings presents on 5 December, not on Christmas Eve. This is because 6 December is Saint Nicholas' Day.

Father Christmas

The tradition of Santa Claus having a white beard and a red suit comes from European stories of an elderly, gift-giving man called Father Christmas. In the Netherlands, the tradition of Saint Nicholas remains strong. When the Dutch settled in the United States, Sinterklaas became Santa Claus. Over time, Father Christmas and Santa have become one and the same.

Ho, ho, ho!

Santa Boots

These little Santa boots will make a cute decoration for Christmas.

1 Place the paper coloured side facing up. Valley fold the paper in half, and then unfold it.

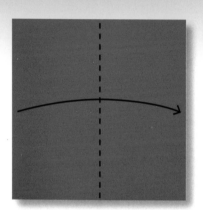

2 Cut the paper in half along the vertical fold line you just made.

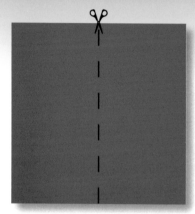

3 Valley fold down the top edges.

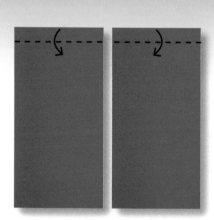

4 Your two pieces should now look like this. Turn the pieces over.

5 Valley fold the pieces in half.

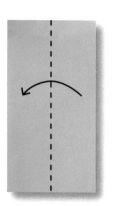

6 Valley fold the pieces in half from the bottom.

26

7 Valley fold the top sections out to the opposite sides.

8 Your models should now look like this. Unfold the last three folds so your models look as they did in step 4.

9 Mountain fold each model piece as shown. To create the shape of the boot, collapse your models. Turn them to the side once finished.

10 Make an inside reverse fold on the top front of the boots to create a toe shape.

Close-up of inside reverse fold

11 Your boots are now complete.

You could also use the boots to decorate Christmas cards and send them to your friends!

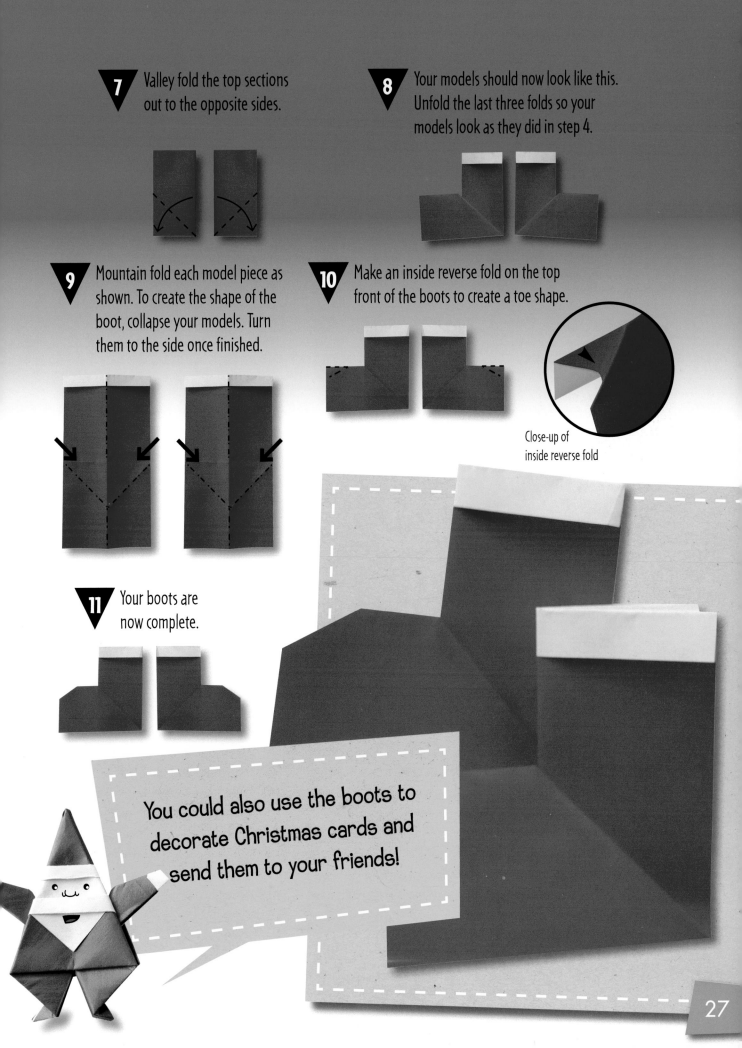

Snowman

In some northern parts of the world, it often snows at Christmas. People build snowmen for fun.

1 To make your snowman, start with a waterbomb base. Valley fold the upper left and right sides into the centre.

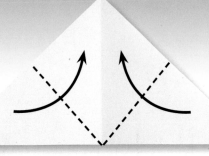

2 Your model should now look like this. Turn your model over.

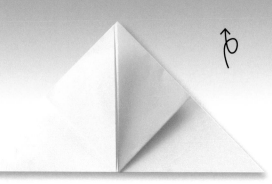

3 Repeat the valley folds from step 1 on this side.

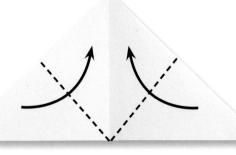

4 Now valley fold the top left and right sides into the centre.

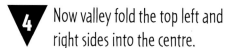

5 Valley fold the top layer of the top points down and slot them into the pockets of the side flaps you just created.

Close-up of points going into pocket slots

6 Your model should now look like this. Turn it over and repeat steps 4 and 5 on the reverse.

7 Your model should now look like this. Blow gently into the small hole at the bottom to inflate your snowman's body. Carefully pull out the sides to help it inflate.

8 Your body is now finished. Repeat with a slightly smaller piece of paper for the head. Attach the body and head with some glue or tape.

Gently hold here

Blow here

Decorate your snowman's face and body with coloured pens or pencils.

Glossary

Advent the four-week period before Christmas Day

angel a spirit found in different religions. Christian's believe that angels are God's messengers and that they protect people

bishop an important religious man of the Christian Church

carols special religious songs sung at Christmas time to celebrate the birth of Jesus

carpenter a person who makes things from wood

custom something that is done often or regularly among people in a particular group or place

evergreen plants that do not lose their leaves in winter

Father Christmas the modern gift-giver at Christmas, whose story comes from old European tales combined with the story of Saint Nicholas

manger a wooden trough used to hold hay or other food for animals

Nativity the story of the birth of Jesus

Saint Nicholas a Christian bishop from the fourth century

Santa Claus the modern gift-giver at Christmas, whose story comes from the story of Saint Nicholas

Sinterklaas the name given to Saint Nicholas in the Netherlands

tinsel a sparkling metallic decoration usually used around Christmas time

tradition something that people of a particular place do often or regularly at a certain time of year

Further Reading

Books

A Christmas Carol: The Holiday Classic, Gently Abridged for Today's Readers, Charles Dickens, CreateSpace Independent Publishing Platform

Easy Origami, Dover Publications

My First Christmas Book, Jane Winstanley, Franklin Watts

Websites

Check out this website to learn how people celebrate Christmas in countries all around the world:
www.santas.net/aroundtheworld.htm

You can find out all about the story of Santa at:
www.stnicholascenter.org/pages/origin-of-santa

There are lots of carols, craft activities, Christmas recipes and much more at:
www.familychristmasonline.com

Note to parents and teachers
Every effort has been made by the Publisher to ensure that these websites contain no inappropriate or offensive material. However, because of the nature of the Internet, it is impossible to guarantee that the contents of these sites will not be altered. We strongly advise that Internet access is supervised by a responsible adult.

Index